BULAKI

Bulaki
Arlene Gurung

Editor: Kallie from Tell Tell Poetry
Photographer: Ujjwal Rana Magar
Cover Design: Kishor Sherchan
Graphic Design: Saman Shrestha

Bulaki

Arlene Gurung

Dear readers,

Before you start reading 'Bulaki', I would like to share a few things with you all. Originally a four-lined poem, unlike my other micro poems, this one always felt incomplete to me. Little did I know that I'd end up writing a mini-book with those four lines. It took me an hour to write this mini book and another hour more to come up with the ideas for the cover and layout design. Once I was done, I had it sent to an editor for proofreading. I found a local publisher that was best suited for me and my self-publishing needs. I was aware about the market for poetry in Nepal being next to none but I was more than willing to take this risk. However, every time we set up a publishing date, something would go wrong. After my third failed attempt to publish this book, I realized that maybe it wasn't the right time yet. After two whole years of waiting and a series of signs from the Universe, the time has finally come. Apart from the inclusion of this letter, every word remains untouched. I have always felt that 'Bulaki' will either be my key to success or my ultimate downfall. This is not just my first book. To me, this book is a part of me that I have been hiding for so long and now, I am finally comfortable enough to share it with you all. This book is not just about me. This book is about every woman who has faced discrimination, inequality, and abuse for being born as a woman. I hope you will enjoy reading this mini book. More than that, I hope you will be able to relate emotionally. Happy reading.

With Love,
Arlene Gurung

Dedication

I would like to dedicate this book to my
great-grandmother,
Mrs. Santa Kumari Gurung
who was an admirable woman.
I grew up listening to her stories from
my grandmother and my mother.
She was indeed a force to be reckoned with.
Hated by few, loved by many
but respected by all.
Thank you for the courage you showed,
the sacrifices you made.
Thank you for raising your daughters
to be strong willed,
who then raised our mothers and aunts
to be brave,
who have now encouraged me and my sisters
to be bold and pave way
for our next generation in line.
We wouldn't have been the woman
we are today, if it weren't for you.
Thank you Ama!

Dear Netra,
Thank you, you saved me just in time.

What better way to silence her than bejewel her with a pure gold, precious, gem-encrusted Bulaki?

We wear this Bulaki to attain heaven's liberation.
But, sadly, this Bulaki we wear has become the symbol of our incarceration.
This Bulaki we wear has taken away our freedom of speech.
This Bulaki we wear has bound us to a life spent on a leash.

Abused and stigmatized, dictated by a male-dominant society.
Crippled and confined, forbidden to reach our potentiality.
Tortured and tormented, at the verge of losing our sanity.
Outcasted and overshadowed, with no rights of our individuality.

Suffocated, we loathe this life under their thumbs.
Their rule was rooted deep within us well before we were born.
This constant pain and suffering, we know where it's coming from.
To this constant pain and suffering, though scared, we will not succumb.

18

I am that woman:
considered not an asset but a liability.

I am that woman:
assumed a lesser being by gender inequality.

I am that woman:
brought home after they weighed her down in a hefty dowry.

I am that woman:
held responsible for their son's demise, untimely.

26

I am that woman:
battered every single day to release his inner frustration.

28

I am that woman:
used as his dangerous secret liaison.

I am that woman:
robbed of her innocence as a child behind closed doors.

I am that woman:
defiled inhumanely on a cold cement floor.

I am that woman:
labeled a freak for being born in a different body.

I am that woman:
branded a sinner for loving a woman profoundly.

38

I am that woman:
abandoned when she was in the midst of creating a new life.

I am that woman:
replaced with someone much younger and more wild.

I am that woman:
sold as a slave, merchandise produced by poverty.

I am that woman:
bought at the flesh market to sate their appetite for carnality.

I am that woman:
kept at a distance because of her so-called untouchable caste.

I am that woman:
humiliated in public for the spells she didn't cast.

I am that woman:
marked a barren land with infertile soil.

I am that woman:
whose refusal led them to make her face boil.

I am that woman:
harassed repeatedly at the workplace and on the road.

I am that woman:
exiled from her family home for being too old.

I am that woman:
banished to a hut for being disgustingly impure.

60

I am that woman:
forced to end her life because she could no longer endure.

I am all of these women; all of these women are me.
I am the voice of these women who have been silenced for centuries.

So let us take off our Bulaki, unseal our lips, and make ourselves heard.
Let us take off our Bulaki. For once, let us be free, not just a flock of caged birds.
No, we will not apologize. And yes, we will scream at the top of our lungs
While we soar the clear blue skies of heavenly space, far-flung.

But before we celebrate, let us go back in time.
A moment of silence to honor all those brave souls who struggled and sacrificed:
Women like us who were destined to be crucified.
Women like us who were destined to be buried alive.
Women like us who were destined to be stoned to death.
Women like us who were destined to be burned at the stake.

The times have changed. Oh, look how far we've come.
We sigh in despair, because there's halfway more.
We sigh in relief, because we're halfway done.
We hope for a better future for our generations to come.
Don't just educate your daughters, let us now educate our sons.
The right of equality begins in our very homes.
The right of equality, be wise and teach them young.
Lay the foundations of the society we've been trying hard to build for so long.
Leave behind a legacy for our daughters and sons to carry on.

70

But my dears,
Should we ever feel like we are all alone,
Should we ever feel like we are not enough:
We dare not give up on us, we dare not give in to self-doubt.
We dare not give in to defeat, dare not give up on the victory we've sought.
We will remember those before us, we will remember the reason they fought.
We will repeat these lines to ourselves until all our dubiety clears out.

Women like us are born to be limitless.
Women like us are born to be fearless.

74

Women like us are born to be admired.
Women like us are born to be empowered.

Women like us are born to be abundant.
Women like us are born to be triumphant.

Women like us are born to be adventurous.
Women like us are born to be courageous.

Women like us are born to be respected.
Women like us are born to be celebrated.

82

Women like us are born to be dreamers.
Women like us are born to be leaders.

Women like us are born to leave a legacy.
Women like us are born to make history.

Women like us are born to be loved unconditionally.
With or without our exquisitely beautiful yet despairingly restrictive Bulaki.

Thou shalt break.
Thou shalt suffer.
Thou shalt rise.
Thou shalt conquer.

To the women before me,
thank you!
To the women after me,
you are welcome!